IDEAS

For Women Only

The Art of a Personal Portfolio

BY HELEN HEIN

Cover Illustration by Linda Jacobus

Copyright © 2015 by Helen Hein

All rights reserved.

ISBN: 978-0-692-47447-1

No part of this book may be reproduced, or stored in a retrieval system, or transmitted in any form, or by any means, electronic, mechanical, photocopying, recording, or otherwise, without express written permission of the publisher.

Printed in the United States of America

CONTENTS

Introduction	5
Chapter 1: Talents	7
Chapter 2: Time Management	11
Chapter 3: Problems and Solutions	15
Chapter 4: Creative Collaborations	27
Chapter 5: The Great Balancing Act	37
Chapter 6: Successful Role Models	47
Chapter 7: Motivation Magic	53
Chapter 8: Self-Discovery	59
Chapter 9: Transforming Moments	63
Chapter 10: The Direction of Your Dreams	71
Chapter 11: Act One: Your Life Story	75
Chapter 12: Hope Chests and Tool Boxes	79
Other Books by Helen Hein	87
About the Author	89
About the Cover Illustrator	91

INTRODUCTION

Ideas…for a more beautiful world.

Ideas, For Women Only highlights the special mission of women in a time that often seems to have forgotten sweetness, light, and a particular way of using talents and strengths as a means of making extraordinary contributions.

At extraordinary contributions, women excel.

In these pages of self-discovery and questioning, as you artfully craft your own personal portfolio—a gift to yourself with a larger purpose—consider these thoughts:

- *I am not afraid…I was born to do this.*
  Saint Joan of Arc, French heroine

- *Great ideas come when the world needs them.*
  Elizabeth Stuart Phelps, American writer

- *This above all: to thine own self be true, and it must follow, as the night the day, thou canst not then be false to any man.*
  William Shakespeare, English poet/playwright, excerpt from Hamlet

Our world needs women. It needs you—your love, your ideas, your uniqueness, your inventions and resourcefulness.

Introduction

You will need a portfolio, some kind of beautiful notebook, journal, or way of recording your answers to provocative questions, planning, and capturing your thoughts. If you embellish it with your personal touches, all the better.

Let's begin…

Chapter 1: Talents

VISION, TALENTS, STRENGTHS

DRUM ROLL PLEASE: YOUR TOP THREE TALENTS

By completing these exercises, you will identify your skills, and learn your top three talents or strengths. If you don't have any idea what your talents/strengths are, ask somebody who knows you well to help you. Here are some questions to get you started. Break in that new portfolio.

1. **What are you good at doing?** How have your talents/strengths been useful or practical in your life? In what ways have they made your life more beautiful? How have your special abilities brought meaning and purpose to your life?

2. **What do you enjoy doing?** Like the bumper stickers, *I'd rather be…* fill in the blank for yourself.

3. **What do people ask you to do?** For example, are you frequently asked to take leadership positions in clubs or organizations? Are you great at decorations or crafts? Do you work well with children? Can you write? Design, sew, or quilt? Speak from a podium? Coach? Do you possess culinary skills? Do you fix or build things? Are you a peacemaker who can assist others in resolving conflicts?

Chapter 1: Talents

Do you throw a great party? Are you a wonderful organizer? Can you sell things, or raise and handle money? What's your thing?

4. **What is your vision of life and your place in it?** Who are you, really? What is the essence of you? Are you a creative person? A logical thinker? An analyst? A religious person? Everybody is good at something. Perhaps you enjoy a physical talent, like the ability to build things. It may be easier to identify tangible rather than intangible skills, like being a singer, but whether tangible or intangible, your skills, talents, or strengths are just as important as anybody else's.

5. **If you had a free day with no "have-tos" on your to-do list, how would you spend it?** This is a very important question, and your answer to it will be revealing.

6. **If you had a free week with no obligations, time that's not a vacation, how would you spend it?** Does this answer speak to the vision you identified in question #4? Next, what about your vacations? Where do you most look forward to going? Do you take big trips, long weekends away, or prefer to stay home? In any of these scenarios, what types of things do you do? What kinds of places do you go on vacation? What are you looking for while you are there? What do your choices say to you? What satisfies you? What brings you joy?

Look back at the questions and your answers. What top three strengths and talents emerge from your responses? Write them down. Commit them to memory. Keep them in mind as you move through your singular life. It's a valuable thing to know yourself and the gifts you bring to the world.

7. **One last thing: consider the past, present, and future applications of your strengths and talents.** Ask yourself how you best utilized your talents and assets in the past; then think about your current situation, and how you might coordinate your efforts and skills now to move your life forward in the direction you wish to go. Align your strengths with your vision for the future, to achieve more of your goals, and you're on your way.

- *Find out who you are and do it on purpose.*
  Dolly Parton, American singer, songwriter

HELPFUL RESOURCE: A self-assessment tool like Gallup's Strengthsfinder program can be useful if you're in doubt about your own strengths/talents. Buy the book and use the code inside to do the assessment online.

You possess gifts that no one else does. The next step is to identify how you want to use your talents, and manage your time accordingly.

- *When we engage in what we are naturally suited to do, our work takes on the quality of play and it is play that stimulates creativity.*
  Linda Naiman, founder of Creativity at Work

Chapter 2: Time Management

TRIPLE WHAMMY TIME MANAGEMENT

People tend to think that time management is primarily about the clock. But it's not.

Time management is primarily about organization and discipline. It's a way of organizing your life and schedule according to your priorities, then taking action on those choices during the time slots you select.

Different people use different systems to organize their time—planners, online applications, daily to-do lists, a master plan broken down into many smaller parts, and the like. Do you have a system in place? If so, what organization system do you use? Is it effective?

Perhaps you utilize more than one method. For example, you might live by a hard copy planner, but also make a daily to-do list. Maybe you prefer an online system, and also keep a set of notes, or a master calendar or planner.

The point is, you must have some kind of system to organize your time, or you will likely forfeit a measure of efficiency and production. When you lose control of your time, you lengthen the time it will take to complete your goals, if they get finished at all.

Chapter 2: Time Management

Choose what works best for you but make sure it includes the following elements. Think carefully about these three areas and be thorough about completing this section. It's extremely important if you wish to develop great time management.

1. **GOALS**: Clarify what you want with pinpoint precision. Name your goals. What is the ultimate goal of your life? What are your secondary goals? What do you hope to accomplish by tomorrow? By next month? By the end of the year? In five years? By the end of your life?

2. **ACTION PLAN**: Develop a simple plan to get what you want. Write an outline for success. Add a timeline. Break it down into manageable parts. What's the next step to achieving your life goals? What's the next step after that? Add implementation details to complete your plan, then prioritize specific tasks that put your plan into action. Simplicity is key. Put things down that you *love* doing and know without a shadow of a doubt that you can do. There is a psychological advantage to seeing a plan committed to paper and saying to yourself: *This is what I want to do. This is what I can do.*

3. **THREE TASKS TO ACHIEVEMENT**: Pick the top task on your list, and do it now. (If you're on a plane, write your action plan.) You can do it. Make sure your tasks are broken down into implementation tasks that are detailed (small and manageable) enough to finish three in a day. Complete the top three tasks of your plan each day, and do them ASAP. Adjust your daily list as necessary. Life does have its hitches, so allow some flexibility. Build into your schedule a day or two off every week to recharge.

Go to work now. Check all three top tasks off in one day, if humanly possible. Do them well, and as efficiently as you can, or you risk not doing them at all. If you work best in the morning, complete your tasks by noon. If you are more of a night owl, do not go to bed until they are done. You know you can do it, and the satisfaction that comes with completing a fine day's work is sublime.

FINISHING TOUCHES. Complete your tasks first, then perfect them. Put the finishing touches on each task when you are done with the preliminary work. Don't get bogged down early. Just get it done, and do it well. Tomorrow has its own work, so complete what needs to be done today—today.

NECESSARY GRUNGE WORK. Remember that no one gets to do 100 percent of what they love to do 100 percent of the time. Some things have to get done just because they are necessary. We're all in the same boat in this, so get things done as they need to be done. The less you like doing it, the faster you work on that task. One-by-one. Check them off. You will love crossing things off that list.

PAYOFF. Now you know what needs to be done, and there is a huge payoff—you edge closer and closer every day to achieving your goals. This is the satisfaction that comes when you finish much of your daily to-do list, every day. Hear that contented sigh? That's you—a happy tired when you sink into bed.

FOR YOUR CONSIDERATION:

- *The first step to getting what you want is this: Decide what you want.*
  Ben Stein, American writer, lawyer, actor, commentator
- *I've learned time management, organization, and I have priorities.*
  Tory Burch, fashion designer, businesswoman, philanthropist

Chapter 2: Time Management

- *Time management is a big part of the director's job.*
  Debbie Allen, American actress, dancer, choreographer, television director/producer.

- *Don't say you do not have enough time. You have exactly the same number of hours per day that were given to Helen Keller, Pasteur, Michelangelo, Mother Teresa, Leonardo da Vinci, Thomas Jefferson, and Albert Einstein.*
  H. Jackson Brown, American author, Life's Little Instruction Book

The next challenge is getting through the struggles, the days when nothing goes right, and the world seems to conspire against you.

Chapter 3: Problems and Solutions

IDENTIFY PROBLEMS / INNOVATIVE SOLUTIONS

Roadblocks. Delays. Interruptions. Everybody has them. Some are unavoidable. Others can keep you from being your most creative, productive self, and serve as a sabotage from you reaching your goals.

When you're struggling, ask yourself big questions:

1. What's the problem? What obstacle is holding you back?

Be honest. Nobody but you needs to know your answer. Just acknowledge whatever it is, so you can begin to either correct it or move on in spite of it. Over time, when you've replaced your worry with success, happiness, and a more enjoyable, creative lifestyle, you can let go of more and more of this roadblock.

If you have more than one obstacle, there is no need to make a big list. Most problems are an offshoot of one or two big ones. If you think you have several things, try to see the bigger picture and condense obstacles to three or less. Less is best.

Here's an example: Procrastination might be a key problem, which could encompass real or perceived contributing factors like: fear of failure, fear of success, shyness, lack of motivation,

Chapter 3: Problems and Solutions

laziness, perfectionism, a cluttered environment, disorganization, and lack of support.

It would be overwhelming and paralyzing for anybody to act in positive ways if a bunch of these factors get in the way at once, so just identify and deal with the one main primary problem—in this example—procrastination. A person can conquer one issue. One is not insurmountable, while nine could be.

The important point to remember is: a person can act even if all the other factors truly do exist. Identify just one problem—the top, primary problem you wish to overcome; the main thing that is keeping you running in place or taking one step forward and two backward. One issue is not an adequate excuse for not moving forward.

Then, complete just one step to tackle the primary problem (a carefully-selected action). In the case of procrastination, it would be one positive action. One. Anybody can do one small thing. Get it done.

After that, take another small step, then another. One by one, as you build momentum, the other factors will begin to fall away. It's the paralyzing non-action that's the problem. Do something positive. Take one small step, but act. Even boulders can be moved with proper leverage, and action.

- *The thing that is really hard, and really amazing, is giving up on being perfect and beginning the work of becoming yourself.*
  Anna Quindlen, American author, journalist, Pulizer Prize winner

- *A journey of a thousand miles begins with a single step.*
  Lao-tzu, Chinese philosopher

- *You never find yourself until you face the truth.*
  Pearl Bailey, American actress and singer

We're all human, and have our own issues, so let yourself up off the mat a little bit. Problems take time to paralyze us, but the fixes can be faster than we think and less overwhelming. Besides, we all stumble and make mistakes. Humility can be a compelling asset. Just pick yourself up and start again. How? Check your to-do list, ask yourself what's next, and simply do that thing. Then repeat. Here's a motivational technique to change behavior fast:

2. Use Positive Habit Triggers.

Triggers can refresh your energy and inspire new, fresh ideas, or solutions to problems. Your biggest problem could be lack of action, or putting your energies in futile directions (Busy work anyone?).

There are many wonderful books out there that offer exercises to jog your memory, light you up, or fill you with renewed interest and energy, but entire books will be useless to you unless they touch on one of your own positive *triggers*. Triggers are what appeal to you, things that excite you and turn on the magical light in your brain, and move you to action. In your personal portfolio, make your own list of triggers. No one knows better than you do what gets you going and puts that sparkle back in your eyes.

Here are a few common positive triggers for you to consider:

a. Put yourself in the company of people that are fun, creative, nurturing, inspiring, and encouraging.

b. Attend a conference or class on your subject matter to get a new and exciting perspective on your area of interest, increase your knowledge, and stimulate your imagination.

c. Read a few pages of a beautiful or interesting new magazine, specific to your tastes.

d. Play music—all kinds. Listen to your favorite music or how-to session for a few minutes on YouTube.

e. Work out. Even if you don't want to, the benefits are unbeatable. It doesn't have to be at a gym. Take a walk at lunchtime. If you don't have that kind of time, then simply step outside for a few minutes of fresh air—rain or shine.

f. Set a goal. For example, if you want a clean house, invite people over. There's nothing like a solid goal and a deadline to get people moving.

g. Go out and see what's new. It could be a museum opening, a favorite boutique or new store, what's playing at a local theater, a concert, new books at a bookstore, the possibilities are endless.

h. Travel someplace you haven't been, or been recently, even if it's only to a neighboring town or community.

Make your own list. Just make sure you don't allow trigger activities to take over tons of your time. You want a trigger that inspires you to complete your own goals, not add a time-wasting, negative, habit trigger to an already busy schedule.

3. Understand Emotional Motivations—Love and Fear

If you don't want to bounce around like a ping-pong ball, it is useful to understand your emotions, and control them, rather than allowing them to control you and your actions.

Many problems can be resolved before they take hold, if you can identify and understand your emotional states, and reasons for behavior—yours and others. Then your response or action is a choice, not a reaction.

The first step in any conflict or strife is to identify your *primary emotions*. Most of the time, our emotions can be plugged into two big, primary categories: Love, and Fear/Hurt.

It might surprise you to discover that anger is not a primary emotion, although it presents itself as one because of its intensity. It's a secondary emotion behind a primary category: fear/hurt.

For example: A young child runs out into a busy street. His mother yells for him to stop. He does, and when she gets to him, she carries him to safety, then sets him down, grabs him by the shoulder, and cries, 'Don't you ever do that again!' The child feels her anger, but what's really going on with the mother is fear that her beloved child could be hurt. If the mother knew what was going on, and could explain it to the child later, he would understand her anger, and realize her love. Instead, he might begin to fear her wrath, and not feel loved at all.

What are your fears? Make your list. Some of the obvious ones are fear of being hurt, fear of pain, fear of failure, fear of success, fear of being alone, fear of not having enough money, and so on. Whatever your fears are, they need attention, day by day. Take inspiration from former First Lady Eleanor Roosevelt, who had many significant and difficult issues to handle during the course of her life:

- *You gain strength, courage, and confidence by every experience in which you really stop to look fear in the face. You must do the thing you think you cannot do.* Eleanor Roosevelt, First Lady

Chapter 3: Problems and Solutions

Sometimes our fears hit a little closer to home.

- *It takes a great deal of courage to stand up to your enemies, but even more to stand up to your friends.*
  J.K. Rowling, British novelist, author of the Harry Potter series

Now for the positives. Who all do you love? Really LOVE. These are the people that you want to spend time with, and can't wait to see.

What do you love to do? What takes no persuasion or outside motivation for you to want to do it? What does your love inspire? Write everything down.

Perhaps love inspires you to marry the person you want to share your life with, and then experiencing life together. Maybe you love having or raising children. Your love could be found in blossoming friendships, or joining a group which shares your sustained interests.

Some people truly love their work. Artists love creating art, and expressing their creativity to bring joy or entertainment to others. Others love innovation, or interacting with people. Many are champions of assisting others, in service occupations. Some thrive in the business world, or in the fields of technology, health care, law, food service, and other lines of work.

- *Work is love made visible.*
  Kahlil Gibran—Lebanese poet, philosopher, and artist

One of the greatest benefits of love is the ability to forgive others. People who have been happily married for a long time know this, or have learned it. Forgiveness is a critical trait to develop for long-term happiness. As long as a person keeps a grudge alive, that person remains wounded.

As the need arises, consider carefully showing forgiveness and mercy to others, and freeing yourself in the process—but take yourself out of harm's way first. Which one of us doesn't need to be forgiven for something? We're human, we make mistakes. Sometimes big ones. So do other people. Forgive. Then forget.

If the thing keeps coming up weeks, months, or years later, then you haven't really forgiven. It could be your pride that is tripping you up, or fear or hurt. Embrace humility by remembering your own faults and weaknesses. Then forgive—and forget. Let whatever it is go and move forward with your life. Life is hard enough without holding onto unnecessary pain.

- *I've had a few arguments with people, but I never carry a grudge. You know why? While you're carrying a grudge, they're out dancing.*
  Buddy Hackett, American comedian and actor

- *Love is all you need.*
  John Lennon, The Beatles

4. Develop Advanced Communication Skills

Communication is a keystone of life.

Many problems in life stem from a lack of good communication skills. Marriages dissolve, friendships end because of misunderstandings, relationships develop strain, families become estranged—all because of poor communication.

Good communication between people creates the opposite: happy, loving marriages; solid supportive friendships; good, working relationships; close-knit, lifelong families.

Chapter 3: Problems and Solutions

The following five communication methods and techniques can help improve communication skills, and relieve a number of life's problems:

a. Engaged Communication

Put down the newspaper, cell phone, and other distractions when someone is talking to you, and listen. Even a child will know if you are only half-heartedly listening. Stop what you are doing when someone seeks you out for a conversation, for advice, or even just to vent.

If someone bores you by rambling on and on, and that's your excuse for tuning out, then do them a kindness. Listen. Recognize that people who spend a lot of time alone tend to chatter a great deal when given a chance.

If it bothers you to irritation, then stop them, and gently note that they're talking a lot about that subject; or respond to them with the point, if you already know it, and that will create a win-win situation. They will feel heard, and you will put an end to the tirade, lecture, or monotonous dialogue.

b. Reflective Listening

When you are trying to improve your communication skills, it is a good practice to learn to listen eighty percent of the time, and speak twenty percent of the time in your relationships. Most people do not have someone to listen to them enough. You be that person.

If you learn to listen to people, you will be considered a great conversationalist. Reflective listening is allowing the person to go deeper and deeper into their topic, and responding to them with the same depth of understanding, while allowing them to lead the conversation to arrive at the answer or insight.

Example Reflective Listening Conversation:

Female: I can't believe he walked out on me during our argument.

Listener: You're upset about that.

Female: Yes, especially when we were discussing getting married.

Listener: You're afraid he doesn't want to get married.

Female: (pausing) He says he does, but…

Listener: He ran.

Female: (Tears in her eyes) Yes, he ran. I love him and he loves me, but maybe not enough. I don't want to get my heart broken again.

The advantage to reflective listening is two-fold. The other person feels valued and understood, and you grow closer to your friend or loved one. People feel safe with someone with whom they can share vulnerable or intimate feelings. If you want great relationships, be that person.

Even in casual social settings, or with acquaintances or business people, you can effectively use reflective listening skills. These conversations will not be as in-depth as those you share with your family, close friends, or loved ones, but they can certainly make a party more fun, and professional relationships and meetings more effective and successful.

c. Open-ended Questions

Open-ended questions are questions that can't be answered with a simple yes or no, or one or two word answers.

These types of questions are great openings at parties and social or business gatherings where you might not know anyone, or catching up with old friends. They invite the other person to talk about themselves, something most people don't get many opportunities to do.

Sample Open-Ended and Simple Response Questions:

(Simple Response/Yes or No) What time will you arrive in Cleveland?

(Response) 11 am.

A dead-end question gets a dead-end answer.

(Open-Ended Question) What will you do when you arrive in Cleveland?

(Response) I arrive at 11:00, and the meeting starts at 6:00 pm, so I'll have time to settle into my hotel. Then, I'll meet up with my co-workers, probably for a late lunch, and we'll go over last minute business preparations before the dinner program begins. It's nice to have a little leeway built into the day. I tend to get jet lag.

You'll get a lot more information with open-ended questions. Listen well, and you'll learn a lot. Your time will come to do the talking. As your pattern of communication improves, so will the communication improve of people you are communicating with, so everyone gains.

d. Empathetic Responses

For everyday problems, most people don't really like sympathy—people feeling sorry, or expressing pity, for them. Sympathy can come across as condescending, or as an acknowledgement of someone's weakness or failure. (Expressing sympathy following a death, accident, or something like that is different; sympathy then is a warm, compassionate response to suffering.)

Generally empathy, when possible, is a better response. It's a closer, more understanding way of providing support, encouragement, or care of another person. It's putting yourself into someone's shoes, and experiencing, so far as possible, their situation, be it happy or sad, success or failure.

    e. Express Yourself

Ask for what you want. Discuss your concerns in a mature fashion. State your reasons for your positions with people who disagree with you. Teach children by example and word. Announce your elation by sharing your good news. Cry if you're sad. Put into words your disappointment. Spread your happiness. Dance if you feel like it. Whistle. Sing. Whatever suits you.

If you learn to communicate well, appropriately, and frequently, then you will less often feel like things are building up to a point of eruption. Nobody appreciates an explosive personality. It causes pain and creates tension, which is not a desirable atmosphere for anyone.

Learn to express yourself in life-giving ways.

- *Speak when you're angry—and you'll make the best speech you'll ever regret.*
  Dr. Laurence J. Peter, Educator and Writer

Chapter 4: Creative Collaborations

At some point it will become necessary to work with others, if you don't already. Collaborations are valuable. They provide a wealth of new, inventive, unusual or unexpected ideas, plus important feedback on how and what everybody is doing currently.

It is desirable to build a network of strong, supportive, and loving people in your life, even if that group is small. Family, friends, colleagues, acquaintances, neighbors, even strangers we encounter, are all part of our community, though not all are collaborations or part of your inner circle. You choose your inner circle.

Healthy Relationships: Like a Magnificent Party

Creative Collaborations. Recognize that many worthy achievements are not products of one, sole effort, but creative collaborations on the part of many. If you've ever been to a magnificent party, you know what I'm talking about.

Take a beautiful wedding, for instance. There is a ceremony to plan, plus additional considerations of accommodating family and friends. Special features may include a beautiful wedding gown, attire for the groom and attendants, seasonal flowers, music, a reception, a photographer, invitations, gifts, a rehearsal dinner, and more—all in some kind of exquisite setting. The bride and groom decide on a whole host of creative collaborations to ensure a lovely wedding, and a happy start to marriage.

Who is in your group of people that you cooperate with for a greater end or goal? This group can and will change with the endeavor.

Collaborations are all about relationships. The healthier your relationships, the more successful your collaborations—so developing a positive network is key.

Healthy relationships are warm, friendly, supportive, reciprocal, fruitful, and loving. They are built on trust and mutual interests. Even in good relationships, people do not always agree with each other, but in circles of healthy relationships, there will always be respect for ideas.

Ask yourself:

1. Who believes in you, no matter what? Who do you believe in, no matter what?

2. Who is committed to you and your success? Whose success are you committed to advancing?

3. Who is your support group, and how do you keep these relationships nurtured? How are you cared for by them?

4. Who shares your special interests? Are you involved in groups, clubs, community organizations, religious affiliations, or professional alliances where your talents and strengths can blossom and grow?

5. Among family or friends, with whom can you safely (without criticism or ridicule) express your ideas, and talk things through?

Collaborations are essential, but then it's time to get to work. Men tend to move more directly toward their creative goals with single-minded devotion. Women tend to enjoy creative diversity, resulting in a rich journey to their goals. Both can be highly effective.

- *The way to get started is to quit talking and begin doing.* Walt Disney, entrepreneur, artist, co-founder of Walt Disney Productions

The following example, *How to Throw a Great Family Reunion,* is a case study of a true-to-life family reunion. It began with an idea that exploded in size and participation.

They thought maybe 100 relatives would attend. A small committee of representatives from four generations of family members helped plan and host a very large and wonderful family reunion, with approximately 270 attendees. They completed a plan with several steps to ensure that the reunion went off without a hitch. By maximizing everybody's talents and interests, they did it! Here's how:

Case Study: How to Throw a Great Family Reunion

1. **Plan, Plan, Plan**. One cousin, who helped on a previous reunion, collected addresses and made flyers. She offered tips on things that went well before, and things that could be eliminated or improved upon. The committee had several planning meetings.

2. **Select Event Dates and Main Activities**. The three days of the reunion went on the calendar. Also the group decided what big meals would be served and where (one big meal each day), and chose activities that would be offered. This began the process.

Reservations were made for the golf course, the community swimming pool, the multipurpose room at the school with a kitchen, and all the other big venues that were necessary for the success of the reunion.

3. **Accommodations.** The group sent out a "save the date" flyer early on (in March for an August reunion), and a list of regional accommodations. The Chamber of Commerce had a list already, so this was easy. The host home town was small, so people were advised to book early, as accommodations quickly filled with this size of crowd.

4. **Communication.** After the initial "save the date" mailing, another two-page flyer went out (in May), and it included an RSVP, a list of activities, and a sign-up sheet for bringing food and ordering t-shirts. All had deadlines and return forms.

The deadlines made it possible to plan menus, approximate attendee number, and allow time to design and pre-order the t-shirts. A "Suggested Donations" line provided the planning group with a budget from which the expenses were paid (i.e., t-shirts, swimming pool fee, trolley fee, janitors, paper products, trapshooting shells, food, etc.).

5. **Coordination of "Gems."** Lots of special touches that family members offered enhanced the reunion experience for everyone.

    a. A family member had a DVD made with old home movies and pictures of the older generation when they were younger, and which included many beloved older relatives, some now deceased. They set it to terrific music, and it was played indoors at the multipurpose room during two main meals. It provided both music and entertainment, and the DVDs were made available to all to take home.

b. Awards, trophies, and engraved medals were preordered to give out at the "awards ceremony" following Saturday's big dinner, for activities and the talent show. All of the children received a prize or trophy or both.

c. An artist cousin designed the t-shirts, another screen-printed them.

d. Four relatives with big personalities became talent show judges, complete with paddles and numbers. One of the guys only gave 10s, which made the contest hilarious.

e. Someone hosted the talent show.

f. Someone took charge of the baseball games.

g. Three young adults got out their laptops and registered all the attendees at the door to get updated contact information (and e-mails) on the computer to make the next reunion easier to plan with improved communication, and to make it easy to send pictures afterwards. A Facebook page was also created, and someone took charge of regular updates.

h. A cousin planned a fantastic outdoor scavenger hunt for children. She had seven teams and included a bag of intriguing goodies and an instruction sheet for each.

i. A family member had done a genealogical study, and brought his spreadsheets to post in the gathering

Chapter 4: Creative Collaborations

multipurpose room for families to update and add their children.

j. Someone brought in two bales of hay, and spread them out on a concrete covered area. Collectively, about $250 in change was thrown in, along with a few special collector coins, and a bunch of wrapped candy, and the children had at it, beginning with the youngest, at appointed times.

k. Four family Alaskan fishermen provided fresh salmon for Saturday's dinner. Another family provided beer. There were many, many contributions like this.

Everyone wanted to help. The spirit of cooperation filled the air. All these were the "gems" of the party.

6. **Set-up and Decorations**. Large banners were ordered to welcome the family and let them know where they could park. There were copies of the event schedules, so people would know when and where to meet for different events. The table decorations were simple, with multiple and colorful long scarves as table runners. Large fresh flower centerpieces were brought in, and smaller flower pots for each table. Engraved shot glasses naming the family reunion and the date were filled with colorful candy and placed on the tables as take-home party favors.

Young adults and teenagers moved tables, chairs, the piano, and did other heavy lifting before and after the event. Two long food tables were arranged to enable the flow of "traffic" so serving would be efficient and easy. Large groups of people could get through four lines quickly.

7. **Photographs**. Three different in-laws offered to take pictures throughout all three days, and they even arranged

a giant family picture in a gym on the bleachers, and different family branch group pictures. The fantastic photographers collectively took close to 3000 pictures over the weekend. They posted on a Flickr account later so all could access them. Someone made a disk for everyone. Also, individuals posted their own pictures on Facebook for everyone to enjoy.

8. **Meals**. For three days of meals and this size of crowd, this task was a chore. The gourmet cooks in the family chaired the food committee, and calculated how much food was needed, including all the traditional family food, and then located where the gaps were, so enough food would be provided.

A cousin then called each of the family branch heads of household and asked their branch of the family to bring a certain quantity of the traditional, cultural food. When the tasks were spread among many, the labors of the individuals were few. The planners also hired a local quartet of women who served and cleaned up after the big meals all three days. These women were lifesavers for the host families, so they could enjoy the party.

THE TWIST—a Progressive Dinner. A progressive dinner on Friday night included four different families, descendants of earlier family members, who happened to live within a comfortable walking distance of each other. All volunteered to host a portion of the progressive dinner, i.e., drinks and appetizers, then salads and bread, followed by the main course at the "family home" and finished at a cousin's home for desserts of homemade pies. The progressive dinner was a smash hit. It began at 4:30 pm with one hour allowed at each home. The weather cooperated, fortunately (not too hot or cold and no rain), and the crowd was staggered enough to not overwhelm each home. A family friend—an artist--offered to open his home (once owned by a forebear) and show his art. This unexpected kindness added additional ease of the big crowd moving from house to house.

Saturday's meal was dinner in the multipurpose room, and a big Sunday morning breakfast provided a nice send-off for travelling families. One sister-in-law made 100 crepes a week for six weeks in preparation of the breakfast, which her family hosted.

9. **Activities.** The key to this reunion's success was to provide enough activities for the children (and all generations of adults) so no one got bored. Then the planners kept to their schedule so things moved along, and started and finished according to plan. This was necessary in order to serve the food on time, keep it hot, etc. A variety of activities were planned, ranging from the progressive dinner, a golf tournament, trolley rides, trapshooting, children's games, a scavenger hunt, talent show, swimming; and poker, bridge, and pinochle games in the evenings, a beer garden at one of the family homes, and a family baseball game with a home run derby for the younger set. (The baseball prizes were signed balls by both of the family's MLB players!)

The grade school also featured a fantastic, elaborate playground that the younger children loved. The school was within easy walking distance of all the family homes and parking there was plentiful.

10. **Event Execution.** There was a point person in charge of each activity, and hosts at each family home. This willingness to step up and take charge is a hallmark of successful family reunions. There were no weak links. The meals and activities went off just as they were supposed to— according to plan. Everybody did exactly what they said they would do and did it well; while others pitched in

wherever they were needed. Everybody was totally spent by the end, but all the effort was worth it.

11. **Evaluation**. On Sunday afternoon, the planning group ate leftovers and discussed each day, reviewing all the elements of the grand three-day party, and savoring the highlights.

Above all, everybody had fun. The party planners showed respect for every organizer, volunteer, and participant, whose talents and efforts became the collective joy of this successful event.

If you build healthy, respectful relationships, and acknowledge and appreciate people's work and efforts, help will arrive when you need it. Embrace the experience and strengths of different generations. The results of *creative collaborations* can be spectacular.

- *No man is an Island, entire of itself; every man is a piece of the Continent, a part of the main.*
  John Donne, English poet, lawyer, and cleric

Chapter 5: The Great Balancing Act

WOMEN: THE GREAT BALANCING ACT

How you define success as a woman will not be the same as how others define success. Your life is like no other. You juggle many roles, some of which may include wife, mother, sister, aunt, friend, grandmother, girlfriend, employee, employer, church-school-community volunteer, pet owner, homeowner, etc. Women today juggle the great balancing act of all time. How well are you managing? Here are a few ways to tap into your best ideas for creating and sustaining harmony in your life, unique to your brain, personality, environment, and beliefs.

Creative Genius

The "Creative Genius" questionnaire is a series of clarification questions. This method is a holistic approach to looking at your life: spiritually, emotionally, mentally, and physically. When each area is in balance, and your life is in order, the opportunity exists for your peak performance. Your subconscious *creative genius* will be ignited. Women have an amazing capacity for achievement, because of already knowing how to get things done efficiently, and often having to multi-task to fit everything into life that they want to do.

Chapter 5: The Great Balancing Act

Forget about perfectionism for this exercise. You are good enough, just the way you are now. Life has enough complications, without any help from us. Already, you have made worthwhile contributions. Seeing ideas through to completion is a complex process, and the more depth your ideas, the more intricate and wide the net you cast, but cast away anyway.

- *Sometimes questions are more important than answers.* Nancy Willard, American novelist, poet, children's author

Answer the questions quickly, and record them in your portfolio. Skim over the questions that have little or no meaning to your life, and tag the ones that do. This is for you alone.

SPIRITUAL: Divine inspiration and guidance, plentiful ideas, being in the flow, unconscious, creative, losing track of time, going beyond where you have been before, allowing new dimensions to elevate your work, experiences, and adventures.

What are your spiritual beliefs?

The last time you felt totally immersed in something productive, what were you doing?

What have you created?

When are you most creative?

When was the last time you counted your blessings? What are they?

What purpose do you serve beyond yourself?

When was the last time you put your talents in service of another? What did you do?

What is the favorite story of your life?

What gives you the most joy in life?

What is the great passion of your life?

Who is your best self?

What are the three most authentic qualities you possess?

What gifts do you share with the larger community, or with the world?

What part of your spiritual being is in association with others?

Is there a communal aspect to your spiritual life? i.e., church worship, charitable event participation, etc.

What groups are you involved with, small or large, where you can discuss spiritual things?

MENTAL: Putting your brain to work with your talents, ideas, thoughts, methods, patterns, aptitudes, your vision for your life. What you know. Your intelligence, where your strengths reside.

If you could do anything right now, what would you do?

Imagine your life as you want it to be.

What was your last innovative idea that improved something, made life easier or simpler, or was effective?

What job or task do you jump right in and eagerly do because you enjoy it?

What do you control in your life?

What is out of your control?

If your voice could be heard around the world, what message would you like people to hear? What wisdom would you share?

Chapter 5: The Great Balancing Act

What's new in your life?

What books have you recently read?

What new ideas or plans have you discussed with others?

What recently has stimulated your imagination in productive ways?

What activities do you participate in with others for mental stimulation?

What groups are you involved in where you can freely share your ideas with others who will support and challenge you?

What is your place in the world?

EMOTIONAL: Your family, friends, coworkers, mentors, neighbors, club and group members, church affiliations, acquaintances, encounters, and media inspirations.

Who do you love to be with? Why?

What do you and your friends have in common?

When you are with friends, how do you spend your time?

What family events are your favorites? Are these large group events, or smaller family gatherings?

Who in your family inspires you? Why?

What time of year tugs at your heart? What is your favorite season?

What qualities do you admire among your friends?

What do you do for fun that involves other people? Do you like social events?

What coworkers, mentors, or acquaintances do you enjoy working or spending time with? Why?

How are you a good friend?

What roles do you play in your family?

How do you develop friendships? Are you a joiner?

What else has an impact on you emotionally? What can lift your spirits? Consider what you like in music...poetry...art...books...movies...travel...blogs...television...sports...concerts...shows...what or who else? Why?

Where do you turn for emotional support? Is it to God? Is it to a person, or to a group of people who share similar aspects of life with you?

If you are involved in an intense group discussion, how do you respond? Are you the cool head of reason, the one who leaves or storms out, the one who stands firm in your convictions, though listening and respecting diverse points of view, or do you take a 'my way or the highway' attitude?

Do you participate in groups in other ways? Are you happy with who you are in group situations?

PHYSICAL: Care of your body, your health, well being, physical fitness, nutrition, sleep habits, energy levels, walks, use and care of the senses—sight, eye and dental care, seeing the beauty around you; hearing lovely sounds, accepting compliments, stimulating conversation, limiting noise and excessive volumes; scents, aroma and fragrance, freshly cut grass; taste, good food, drink; touch, touching another, another touching you, textures.

The last time you were bold physically, what did you do?

How do you like to exert yourself?

How often do you notice a physical or tactile reaction, like the warmth of the sun on your skin, the cold of the snow, plunging into cold water, immersing into a hot bath or hot tub, the feel of sand through your fingers, drifting off to sleep, waking up after sleeping?

What do you physically plan to do in the next hour? Next week? Next month? Next year? The next five years?

When did you last experience and enjoy nature?

In what ways do you exercise your body and keep it fit? How regularly?

How do you relax?

Do you get enough sleep?

Are you often sick, or are you most often well? If you are chronically ill, how do you maintain a positive approach to your physical well being?

How do you show respect for your body? Do you accept it the way it is now?

Do you participate in a team sport or group activities, like hiking? Did you ever? If yes, what good things did you gain from these experiences? What took away from the positive things?

Have you worked in conjunction with others on a physically taxing joint effort, such as building a house, a fence, a boat, or other structure? Would you repeat that experience? Why or why not?

Are you comfortable with your body when you look in the mirror? Are you comfortable with your body when in the presence of others? Does it make any difference? Why or why not?

A healthy lifestyle is a natural balance of all these areas, but sometimes, as you well know, it can be a wacky world, and many parts in it can be quite a lot out of balance. Sometimes a major project is consuming until it is finished. That is okay too, and necessary on occasion, but take care not to stay in obsession zone too long, for your own health and those around you. If you're tired, rest. You're going for optimum health and productivity here, and if you burn out, that's not it.

Generational Motivations

People of different generations work differently, and each method can bring fantastic results. Tap into the intelligences of all generations for insights from different perspectives, and keep up with technology as much as you need to for best results.

Anticipate Change

Change is a given. Each day you are a day older. Life changes. Skills can become outdated or obsolete. Life choices impact careers. Yet ideas, and the ability to innovate will not ever become obsolete. Skills can be reinstated, updated, and polished.

Creativity and Women

In research on creativity and women, education or lack of education did not impact female creativity, nor did personality factors. Women can be quiet or enthusiastic, calm and reserved or eccentric and laugh a lot. What traits do creative women all have in common? These are: creative energy, vitality, intensity about life and work, satisfaction and contentment in life.

Chapter 5: The Great Balancing Act

- *Success is getting what you want; happiness is wanting what you get.*
  Ingrid Bergman, Swedish actress

Women and Creative Choices

Women thoughtfully make creative choices that may change or weaken their career paths or salary levels, but which in fact, may advance and strengthen society. For example, many women choose to have a family, though raising children may take time away from career progression and opportunities. Motherhood becomes one of their vocations.

A female sculptor put it this way: "I have spent the last 25 years sculpting my three children. They have taken every ounce of my creativity." Many women believe that their family collaboration of raising children, whatever the sacrifice, is their best contribution of all to make a positive difference in the world.

It is possible to have more than one vocation. Women around the world manage it every day. What creative choices are you making?

Valuable Skills of Women

Women who choose to have children and delay their careers in some way, can prepare for future work in other ways. They can do community service; as volunteers they develop programs and put them into practice, take leadership positions, and use their talents to better society.

For example, web experts can build websites for community groups, volunteers can accept leadership positions, composers can start bands or write for one, poets can teach children the joy of writing poetry, artists can be docents at a school, or show their work in galleries, etc. All these types of skills—and many others—help women move forward in their careers, and skills can be packaged and marketed professionally. Whether at home raising families or coming up with innovative ideas at work, women are capable of long-term commitments to their creative potential. Often, these creative paths go outside the norm, because each woman is different, and has different needs for her life.

What creation or idea must express itself "outside of the box" at your home? At your work? In your volunteer activities and/or charitable work? How does this contribute to maintaining balance in your life?

- *An artist paints, dances, draws, writes, designs, or acts at the expanding edge of consciousness.*
  Julia Cameron, American writer, artist, filmmaker

- *Around here...we don't look backwards for very long. We keep moving forward, opening up new doors and doing new things, because we're curious...and curiosity keeps leading us down new paths.*
  Walt Disney, co-founder (with his brother Roy) of Walt Disney Productions.

Chapter 6: Successful Role Models

WHAT'S YOUR FAVORITE SUCCESS STORY?

Successful Role Models

Who are the most successful people (not famous) that you know and admire?

What is it that you like about them?

What special trait or attribute do they possess that symbolizes their success?

For example, someone could have a larger-than-life personality, or be stylish and chic, or perhaps be deeply prayerful and peaceful. Others may be go-getters, risk-takers, or highly creative and prolific. All could be successful in some ways, and not in others.

Who do you consider a successful role model for your life and dreams, goals, and purpose? Why?

What's your favorite success story?

Famous Names

What famous people, past or present, do you consider successful? Why?

What obstacles did your successful men and women have to overcome to achieve their objectives?

Learn their stories. Your biographical research (the internet is a great tool) might provide a few surprises. Not everyone's life is as glamorous as it looks. Other people may be even more noteworthy than you realized.

Did the people you chose spend time working for a cause beyond their fame? Perhaps they were philanthropic in some area, or maybe a volunteer or spokesperson for a group?

After learning more details about their story, are they still successful to you? Do you consider them worthy role models? Why or why not?

Mini Interviews

Want to know how to do something? How someone negotiates? How to develop a special skill? Ask your family, friends, and acquaintances questions about what you want to know that they know.

Most people do not get the opportunity very often to talk about what they do best or know a lot about, and many of them will be happy to spill their secrets to you. Let people closest to you share their life stories and creative successes, and you will discover how they did it, and what motivated and propelled them to success.

Ask open-ended questions that speak to their interests, and yours, and then listen. These are valuable conversations, and if you're a good listener who doesn't interrupt, you will get the answers you seek, and maybe a few secret ingredients for success as a bonus.

Research

Read various publications and books. Use the internet wisely and be discerning about what you read. Observe and talk to people from your community, at parties, in stores, at your workplace, school, or neighborhood. Research is like getting the combined intellect of many for virtually free.

Find the Brilliance

Think well of people. Find their intellectual assets. Avoid judging people based on their appearance, apparent skill level in certain things, or lack of skills. They may be brilliant in some other area. Everybody has a valuable story. If you appreciate diversity and learn from it, you will add new ideas, techniques, or ways of doing things to your repertoire.

Deal-Breakers

What's your strong suit? Identify your best method of working.

Is it fast? Detailed? Thorough? Fine-tuned? Aesthetically pleasing? Do you have an innate understanding about situations that baffle others? Do you keep your head in a crisis? Are you good with people? Do you work harder and care more? Are you known for your integrity? What makes you a go-to person for others?

What demands on your time are absolutely necessary for your health and well-being? What choices are you consciously making now that are sacrifices for you, but you wouldn't have it any other way? In what ways do people count on you (and you deliver)?

What are your deal-breakers? What are you willing to do to succeed, and what are you not willing to do? These types of things are powerful, and they say something important about your character and values.

Your People

Consider your network of people.

Can you trust the people you love, even with your dreams? Do you know who gossips? Be aware in order to discern what you share and don't share.

Who do you turn to for support and feedback? Who are your Facebook friends? Whose posts on Facebook do you enjoy, and whose do you hide? What people can you not live without? Who enriches your life?

Helpful (and not so helpful) People

Most women have friends or family who help them to live more fully and be better human beings, but not always in every area. People serve different purposes in our lives, as we do in other people's lives. Spend as much time as possible with nurturing, positive, supportive people, and do your best to be one of these people for others.

A note about hurtful people: most people have a person or two in their lives with toxic or obnoxious personalities, behaviors that hurt them, or exorbitant neediness that drain them to the last drop. Some of these encounters are unavoidable, but do your best to keep the negative influences to a minimum. Damage control as much as possible, especially if the situation is chronic and there is no movement towards improvement. It's self-preservation to protect yourself and your family.

If the situation simply can't change at this time, then try to find the good in people and focus on that. Everybody has some redeeming quality; there is usually a flip side to every coin, but still minimize time with people and things that disturb your peace and trouble you.

Overwhelm With Kindness

Be a nice person. There is joy in being a kind and happy person, with beautiful ideas and creativity that flows and overflows. Positive, creative people are very hard to hate, and negativity pings off them, because their love of beauty and goodness is their shield. Be the person who enjoys life, and finds joy in others.

Take a few minutes and add some joy and personalization to your growing portfolio. Write in some of your reflections. Put in a few beautiful, special, and memorable thoughts or things to it that make it a pleasure to open.

- *You can't use up creativity. The more you use, the more you have.*
Maya Angelou, American author and poet

Chapter 7: Motivation Magic

Motivation. This concept is much written and talked about, but what is it really? Simply put, motivation is why we do what we do.

It sounds easier than it is in reality, but the more you understand your motivation or lack of motivation for doing or not doing something, the more your choices become apparent to you. Then, whether you do something or not is a conscious decision, and not some vague procrastination.

- *A person often meets his destiny on the road he took to avoid it.*
  Jean de la Fontaine, French fabulist and poet

- *They don't remember what you try to teach them. They remember what you are.*
  Jim Henson, puppeteer, film director, television producer (Muppets)

Motivation in Business: Some businesses provide positive rewards and incentives to motivate employees to develop passion and drive to meet company goals and improve performance: things like salaries, benefits, cash bonuses, trophies, trips, or praise. These are all external motivators. They can be successful in spurring people on to meet goals outside of themselves, such as company sales objectives.

Conversely, there can be negative consequences to do or not to do something too, that can cause avoidance or fear. For example, not meeting sales quotas could result in job loss, demotion, or poor performance reviews.

Once in a while, especially with a new product or service, sales may far exceed goals. It's more rare, but exciting when it happens.

- *Do just once what others say you can't do and you'll never pay attention to their limitations again.*
  James R. Cook, British explorer and navigator

Personal Motivation: What personally motivates people is their interests. It's their predisposition to do things that they like doing. There is no need for external pressure for action. Personal interests already fill their needs, so people want to do them, and they do not have difficulty persevering in what they love to do. These are internal motivators.

Usually people are very good at their personal motivators. They have competence and even perhaps a drive and intensity about them, and they move people forward to their desired outcomes. With personal motivations, there is also the freedom of autonomy: people do what they want, when they want to do it.

Sometimes other people can relate to what motivates us, because it motivates them too, and communities are developed around that interest (i.e., quilting, music, art, sports). This community can result in exceptional productivity and happiness in the process.

Once in a while you might hear the expression, *you were born to do this*. These are empowering words, and they sometimes result in positive changes in people's behavior and commitment. This is a positive reinforcement of personal motivation.

- *You can't just sit and wait for people to give you that golden dream. You've got to get out there and make it happen for yourself.*
  Diana Ross, American singer, actress, and record producer

MOTIVATION MAGIC

Motivation is usually correlated with some type of creativity.

For example, making a sale requires building a relationship of some kind, giving a pitch, and closing the deal. Salespeople are frequently highly creative in overcoming objections, giving sales presentations, striking a deal, and other qualities that require thinking on their feet. They may also be creative in handling inevitable rejection.

Developing something innovative and creative often can be a lonely, solitary activity, with or without a lot of encouragement from others for your ideas. Here are ten tips that can work magic in moving an artist, writer, or creator (of any kind) to action:

1. Warm up with a small project that is easy to complete for quick results. This builds momentum. Then stop for a time, continue working, or sketch or develop drafts of the next project. Try to leave your work somewhat open-ended, so you can start right in when it's time to return to it.

2. Try a cool new tool or technique and see where it goes.

3. See creativity as a body of work, a repertoire or portfolio that increases over time. Keep adding to it, and look it over from time to time. As a result, a certain personal style will emerge, unique to the artist or creator. It will seem to have blossomed as effortlessly as the sun comes up in the morning. People will begin to say—*that looks*

like you, that sounds like you. In the business world, this is personal branding.

4. Watch how small children play, eat, or interact with others. They discover exciting things out of ordinary surroundings. Their imagination gives new meaning to trees, rocks, sticks, grass, flowers, water, dirt, leaves, creatures, playground equipment. Like a child, abandon for a while preconceived notions about things and see the ordinary in sensory ways, such as textures, shapes, colors, fragrance, sounds, rhythm.

5. Drive to someplace special, rural or urban, perhaps a place not seen before. Photograph, sketch, or note what's best about it. Look for poetry, harmony, or contrast in the surroundings. Notice the specialness of the current season in nature.

6. Experience a farmer's market, flea market, local festival, art show, concert, library, museum, or sidewalk sale. Load up on themes, trends, excitement. Enjoy the visual feast. Take notes and pictures. Pick up postcards and samples of appealing things.

7. Before bed, prepare your workspace for the next day. Check your planner, gather supplies, fill your proverbial paintbox, with paper at the ready, and sharpen your pencil. In the morning, everything's ready to go.

8. Realize that everybody has exactly the same amount of time in their day as everyone else, even the President of the United States. Use time wisely.

9. If you feel lonely, play music and sing for company, take a class in person or online, work with someone on a project, show new work to a supportive friend or family member.

Pick up the phone and call someone. Remember that no one is really alone. Artists, writers, and creators of all kinds are coming up with something new and beautiful this very minute. Consider yourself in a universal collaboration for a good and positive effect in the world.

10. When possible, work jointly with other people, to brainstorm ideas, get and give feedback, and generally provide support and encouragement for one another. A mastermind team can be very productive and useful.

Peak Performances

There's more than one way to achieve creative success.

Here's a creativity fact: men's creativity tends to peak early; women's creativity tends to peak late. In fact, women over 50 are entering a dramatically creative time of their lives, so don't discount maturity.

Whatever the age, shed the cultural and societal values that devalue women because historically they are not the highest achievers and producers in salaries or world prizes. Some of our greatest poets and artists died without recognition or many resources during their lifetimes. Change the present and the future and value the positive contributions of women.

Research shows that men often compartmentalize all the pieces of their lives, but women hold them all at once, honoring each as they go through life. Women work professionally, they bear and raise children (giving life is very high on the creativity scale), volunteer, support charitable causes, care for elderly parents, sustain friendships, and make many sacrifices, personally and professionally, to meet and sustain all these commitments, and still strive to work at peak performance.

- *Whatever women do they must do twice as well as men to be thought half as good. Luckily, this is not difficult.*
  Charlotte Whitton, Canadian politician, Mayor of Ottawa

- *There is nothing like returning to a place that remains unchanged to find the ways in which you yourself have altered.*
  Nelson Mandela, former President of South Africa, anti-apartheid revolutionary, philanthropist

CREATIVE JOY, PURE JOY

If you want creative joy: put in the sparkle. Add finishing details and touches. Other people may not notice specific things, just that there's a fullness or richness about the work. Go the extra mile. These efforts are palpable to others—and sometimes they can really be something.

- *Few people take objectives really seriously. They put average effort into too many things rather than superior thought and effort into a few important things. People who achieve the most are selective as well as determined.*
  Richard Koch, British author, speaker, and investor

Personal Portfolio Ponderings. What are your key motivations? Why do you do what you do? What motivates you in your business or professional life? What are your external motivations? What are your personal motivators or internal motivators? What is the motivation magic that inspires you to creative joy? What stymies your progress? What helps you achieve your peak performance?

Chapter 8: Self-Discovery

- *Men go abroad to wonder at the heights of mountains, at the huge waves of the sea, at the long courses of the rivers, at the vast compass of the ocean, at the circular motions of the stars, and they pass by themselves without wondering.*
   St. Augustine, Christian theologian and philosopher

Self-discovery is about wondering. It's a process of discovering how you feel about life's big questions, about spiritual issues, and priorities. It involves examining your thoughts and ideas, and incorporating the best of things learned in your years into your own personal philosophy. Self-discovery is identifying what you believe and don't believe. In this clarification of values, you discover who you are, and what the essence of life is for you.

Take some notes about yourself on all these subjects, and form a personal philosophy of your own.

Think about your own sense of self. How would you describe yourself as you are now? How would you want to describe yourself in 10 years? What kind of journey would it take to get from here to there?

Also important: identify what makes you happy, what makes your heart sing, and how you define greatness.

Chapter 8: Self-Discovery

- *It's a helluva start being able to recognize what makes you happy.*
  Lucille Ball, American actress and producer

- *Let your heart guide you. It whispers, so listen carefully.*
  Littlefoot's mother, Land Before Time

- *Keep away from people who try to belittle your ambitions, small people always do that, but the really great make you feel that you, too, can become great.*
  Mark Twain, American author and humorist

Self-Discovery Moments

Sometimes self-discovery comes to us by way of an insight from someone else. Once in a while, it may even be a gift from a total stranger. Consider this story:

On a city sidewalk in broad daylight on a warm summer day, the young woman walked slowly, deep in thought over a serious and unsuccessful meeting she had just finished. As she studied the ground, contemplating what to do next, a tall, good-looking, bearded homeless man broke her concentration when he spoke to her. 'What are you so happy about?'

She glanced up in surprise that he addressed her with sarcasm, but also a bright smile. Her eyes met his for a brief moment. She couldn't help but smile in response. There was something light in his eyes, and an abiding gentleness in his countenance.

Dignity.

He sauntered along with ease and a total lack of concern about himself. His clothes, though ragged, fit him well, and he managed style though apparently lacking money. As he passed her shoulder to shoulder, he turned his head towards her and pausing for a second, he acknowledged her smile by saying 'That's better,' and passed on by. This man did not have his hand out for anything; he gave her a gift instead.

After the man walked on, the young woman saw the beauty around her in that moment. Later, she would notice the sunny day on the waterfront, and lunch at her favorite café with her supportive young husband. Even in her disappointment, she had a lot to smile about.

When the homeless man died, someone posted a small picture and obituary of 'The Gentleman Beggar.' John—his name— never left the streets, but others obviously had similar experiences in encountering this special man.

In the big scheme of things, it was a small moment in this young woman's life, but a big lesson. In her self-concern, she failed to realize the impact she had on others, even a stranger on the street. The mirror the homeless man held up to her was not cruel or mean-spirited, but constructive and effective. In a small way, he did her a great kindness.

Self-Discovery Windows

Imagine two neighboring windows close together, facing each other. They are open. You are standing at one of them, and your best friend is standing at the other, facing you. You can see each other from the waist up, where the window starts.

Your best friend's window represents what you know about yourself and everybody else does too (your friend sees your hair color, your height, your demeanor). Your friend's window also represents what she and others know about you that you do not know about yourself, great things and not-so-great things (for example, you have an engaging smile and wonderful eye contact that make you very approachable; but you may also have a nervous habit of laughing).

Your window represents what you know about yourself that others do not know, or that you do not want them to know (for example, you love to dance; or you have a fear of public speaking).

What can your best friend teach you about yourself? What traits or characteristics do you have that are appealing to others? How can what you learn about yourself from others benefit you? What do you know about yourself that you could better utilize?

For this technique, use only your best friend, who loves you and wants the best for you. This isn't an exercise in criticism, it's to recognize and enhance your attributes, and adjust easily correctable tendencies, so you present yourself in the world to your best advantage.

As your moments of self-awareness increase, so will your ability to see and understand your behavior more clearly.

- *There are chapters in every life which are seldom read, and certainly not aloud.*
  Carol Shields, Pulitzer Prize-winning author

- *While we have the gift of life, it seems to me the only tragedy is to allow part of us to die—whether it is our spirit, our creativity or our glorious uniqueness.*
  Gilda Radner, actress, comedienne

Chapter 9: Transforming Moments

What are some of your life's best moments, the moments that changed your life in some wonderful way? What do you consider your greatest successes? Was anybody with you? Did anybody change or grow? Did you?

The following short story, entitled *Two Minutes of Heaven*, is about just such moments. Enjoy.

TWO MINUTES OF HEAVEN

My socialite mother and my new husband had a cool, aloof relationship, resembling disdain, until one special morning...

They didn't like each other very much. Not from the beginning, and not even after a few months. My mother, Jackie, and Scott, my husband of one year, had never exactly hit it off. You could probably even accurately describe their relationship as contentious.

My parents live in a nearby city, so while we see them fairly frequently, we aren't in each others' pockets. Still, this in-law mutual friction between Mother and Scott only heightened when I announced my pregnancy. Scott, elated, couldn't wait for the sacred event, and Mother, at forty-nine, felt put out to the extreme to become a grandmother at such a young age.

Chapter 9: Transforming Moments

I'm twenty-three, and she thought I had oodles of time to start my family, and that I should have waited. Scott, at thirty-three, couldn't have disagreed with her more, and besides, as he noted, it was none of her business.

In my ninth month, my mother faced facts, and became accustomed to the idea of a baby in the family. Embracing layette shopping as a matter of familial duty, she in her usual manner of excess, went way overboard, supplying us with every useful and nonsense item ever produced for the younger set. The fabulous baby quilt she found, however, I will treasure forever.

"Doesn't she think I can support my own family?" Scott grumbled as he surveyed the latest loot in the nursery. By all accounts except Mother's, Scott was a business success—albeit blue-collar—which was, sadly, the cause of her chagrin and discontent with her only child's spouse.

It's a bit easier to understand this prejudice when you're born with a silver spoon in your mouth as I was, but nevertheless, in my case the social status intolerance just didn't take. I love my carpenter. Wildly. Nobody on earth could have kept us apart. Robert, my dad, loves him too, and that fact made the "bringing him home to meet the parents" step infinitely easier. It's also fortunate that my down-to-earth father kept me from being too awfully spoiled rotten and biased. In fact, Dad was my hero, right up until I met Scott, and though my father didn't get dismissed in the love department, he did get usurped as hero.

Today I realized why it was such an easy, graceful transition of knight-in-shining-armor-hood from Dad to Scott. The two men are just plain alike. It frightened me, I admit, to also discover that in some ways, I take after my mother as well. In looks, this similarity is a blessed thing, because she's a beauty, and age has only increased this marvel, but her somewhat stuffy personality and uptown attitudes are a tad bit scary for my decidedly laid-back country tastes. On occasion I have been known to interrupt myself with a mental swift kick when I catch a phrase of pomposity escaping my lips. What a puffball I used to be—and still am—now and then. Scott very gently helps me with this. I sincerely hope I'm improving.

As they sometimes do, these things all came to my attention at once in a burst of awareness.

Shortly after the birth of my darling baby boy, on a crisp November evening, I had an open house at my fledgling, small town boutique to introduce an abundance of holiday selections. I feared that I had overspent my wad and overextended my energies, but once in a while, some unexpected happy thing takes place, as it did this night.

My open house turned out to be a full-blown social event, and Mother came to my rescue. With her interior design background, she became invaluable to me like never before. In short order, my little store looked sensational. Mother transformed my rickety building, artfully covering the cracked wall with a golden Christmas tree brimming with elegant ornaments, and she disguised the worn carpeting with an elaborate layering of merchandise, giving the space such dimension and color that no one noticed where they stepped because the eye was drawn elsewhere to something beautiful.

As if this wasn't enough, her window displays beat all. Mother dressed a winter scene up in velvet and lace, in a manner befitting a grand old mansion, deserving of tender care and respect. My mother and I wore long, luscious gowns for the occasion that were eye-popping for our casual, dressed-down husbands to view. Each and every woman who came to the store visibly relaxed as she walked in the door, greeted by us with a handshake or hug and a cup of hot apple cider. By eight, a regular party of women had gathered, sipping and chattering, enjoying the gentle music of the harpist I hired for the evening, the warm ambience of the many candles we had lit, and each other's company as they wandered through the store, touching and pointing at things.

I tired quickly, the unhappy result of getting up a time or two every night with my angel baby. Frankly, I was downright sleep-deprived and edgy. Rising to the occasion however, Mother took over the bulk of my hostess duties with infinite finesse, and proceeded to sell a small fortune worth of merchandise. This thrilled me, as much as my irritable disposition would allow, and I lavished profuse praise and my undying appreciation on her.

Did I mention that Mother brought a few of her wealthy friends from the city to indulge their passion for shopping at my store that very evening?

I knew the open house truly succeeded when I saw my back room stock totally depleted. Utterly exhausted by eleven when Mother mercifully walked the last, leisurely, night-owl customers to the door, I flipped the sign to CLOSED, PLEASE COME AGAIN. I gained new respect for Mom that evening, and fell asleep while extolling her exceptional virtues to my skeptical husband.

The next morning, however, blew my mind.

Babies are simply gorgeous little people, never accountable for waking up their mothers to nurse in the middle of the night or in the early hours of the morning. This morning was no different, only I was even more incoherent than usual because of my late and busy evening. Bobby, my beloved infant in fresh diapers, howled, as I, in my once-beautiful bathrobe, now showing signs of too many washings, carried him to the kitchen bar and slid gingerly into a chair to nurse yet again.

My precious husband ably built a cozy fire, then loitered near the toaster, feebly attempting to help my dad who had commandeered the kitchen to cook breakfast. Scott gratefully turned to observe his little family and smiled as he leaned down and slid his arms across the counter to us. "Lisa, honey, it should be a crime to look as good as you do in the morning without any sleep," he murmured in his low, deep voice filled with love.

Did I mention that my drop-dead handsome husband, who is virtually useless in the kitchen, is also exceedingly charming?

Suddenly, without any warning, it happened. Dad burst into song. Now, he has a nice voice, but not a great one. This day though, on a cold, rainy, early winter-like dawn, his singing sounded spectacular, and he chose of all things, a beach song! A surf's up type of number! I stole a glance at my mother across the room to gauge her reaction, and she looked nonchalant, busy working counting the proper number of place settings for our meal, while here was Dad, singing about the sun, the beach, and love at the top of his lungs. He sang and danced with total abandon, shimmying over to the breakfast table with a plate of steaming bacon and sausage, where Mother didn't just set our plain Jane table, she prepared it as a thing of beauty, complete with exotic touches of branches and leaves she had collected earlier in the morning.

As Dad sidled up to her, singing and grinning about being on a blanket with his baby, he kissed the back of her neck. Mother, not terribly prone to overt displays of affection, smiled and kissed him back. Wonder of wonders! I think I even heard her giggle for a second or two. It was enough to melt an iceberg, and that wasn't all.

Duly inspired, my own husband, with an even more mediocre voice than Dad's, chimed in spontaneously to contribute harmony; his pathetic, off-key baritone offering the refrain. He is

Chapter 9: Transforming Moments

however, an incredible dancer, and this redeeming quality saved him from hilarity as he sensuously weaved his way around the breakfast bar to me and Bobby, gently cradling our baby's head as he moved, and stroking my cheek ever so tenderly. Bobby moved his head for a brief time to croon aloud too, and together my men made the most beautiful sounds that I've ever heard in the world.

It was two minutes of heaven, then it ended.

The song was over, the doorbell rang, and Mother's friends all piled into our smallish apartment for breakfast, while baby and I fled for the privacy of my bedroom to finish the feeding we started and to make ourselves presentable for company.

From that morning on, something perceptibly changed in the relationship between my mother and my husband. Perhaps they each gained a deeper appreciation for each other's finer qualities, or maybe Dad simply brought out the best in us all by his great joy of life and complete lack of inhibition.

Whatever the case, I'll never forget those priceless moments, when three generations of a family melded into a seamless one—of love.

* * *

Life's transforming moments seem to arrive when we least expect them. Lay your groundwork, keep moving forward in positive ways, and when they show up, you'll be ready for them.

- *Love is the only force capable of transforming an enemy into friend.*
  Martin Luther King, Jr., American pastor, civil rights activist, humanitarian

- *Do not suppress it–that would hurt you inside. Do not express it—this would not only hurt you inside, it*

would cause ripples in your surroundings. What you do is transform it.
This is the way of peace: overcome evil with good, and falsehood with truth, and hatred with love.
Peace Pilgrim, born Mildred Norman, American non-denominational spiritual teacher, peace activist who walked more than 25,000 miles for peace

- *An invasion of armies can be resisted, but not an idea whose time has come.*
  Victor Hugo, French poet and novelist

Chapter 10: The Direction of Your Dreams

WHERE DO YOUR DREAMS TAKE YOU?

Your Biography: Heading in the Direction of Your Dreams

Write a brief biography of your own life so far. Give a sense of place and time in your childhood, with your family, friends, schools, activities, etc. then take yourself through the other stages of your life to the present moment. State all the pertinent facts about yourself (like you might read in an internet biography).

Then go beyond this basic description. Decide for yourself what your place in the world is as you see it. What is the meaning of your life? Where do your dreams take you? How would you like to be remembered? When you've finished writing your answers in your personal portfolio, put it aside for a while, then come back to it and read it through.

Does anything surprise you? Do any patterns emerge that have become prominent without your realizing it? Are you heading in the direction of your dreams?

Your Dreams

After you've completed your biography, and have a strong sense about yourself from your past and present, now think of the future. What is the deepest dream and dearest hope of your life? Are you living your dream now? Are you partially living your dream? How are you stepping towards that dream?

If your dream is still a fantasy, what elements can you take from your fantasy life and apply to your present and future? Are there qualities in your hopes and dreams that you already possess? Our dreams have something to teach us about ourselves. What are yours telling you?

- *The future belongs to those who believe in the beauty of their dreams.*
  Eleanor Roosevelt

You're Driving

On my first major road trip when I was a teenager, I traveled by car with one of my older brothers and two older sisters from Washington to California. It was summer, and we were in a car with no air conditioning, so the windows were all down, and the wind rushing into the car created significant noise. I had just earned my driver's license, but as a new driver, I didn't take a turn at driving all the way down to our destination.

On the trip home, my brother decided it was time for me to take the wheel. We were small town kids, and I had only driven on the freeway once before, and then, only briefly. I was a timid driver, because at eleven, I had been a passenger in a major car accident, and had developed a fear of driving with passengers in the car with me.

Still, I took the driver's seat, and drove rather unsteadily for a while. I could feel the stress from my sisters in the back seat, but my calm brother sat in the passenger seat by me, and took the situation in hand. He told me I was dovetailing—looking just ahead of the hood of the car, so the back end of the vehicle was swerving back and forth. He said to try looking farther down the road so I wouldn't be so jittery with the steering wheel.

I did as he directed, and voila, it worked! My driving was much smoother. He acknowledged my improvement. I realized that the freeway was just another stretch of road, and as I began to relax, my sisters began to chat and sing again, and my turn at driving was uneventful, a good thing.

I learned two things that day: It's good to see farther down the road sometimes. Seeing the bigger picture can help calm the present.

The second thing is that the time will come when you will be in the driver's seat, and there can be real pleasure in having that portion of control. Being in control of your actions plays an important role in your destiny.

Life Vision Road Map

Imagine a spreadsheet or large road map of your own life vision. Perhaps it resembles a collage or a game board. If you're a visual thinker, then draw it. Sketch it out. What do you want your life vision to look like? How will you make a difference? You were born for a reason. What will be your lasting legacy? How will you leave the world a better place?

Go in the direction of your dreams. Trust your heart in your work. Immerse yourself in the adventure of ideas and creations, then offer the world your best, most awesome work yet. Let your life vision guide you. Start where you are right now and move forward.

- *Start by doing what's necessary; then do what's possible; and suddenly you're doing the impossible.*
  St. Francis of Assisi

Chapter 10: The Direction of Your Dreams

- *Thank goodness I was never sent to school; it would have rubbed off some of the originality.*
  Beatrix Potter, English author and illustrator of children's books

- *In the end, it's not the years in your life that count. It's the life in your years.*
  Abraham Lincoln, 16th President of the United States

Chapter 11: Act One: Your Life Story

HOW DOES YOUR LIFE STORY LOOK IN LIVING COLOR?

- *All the world's a stage, and all the men and women merely players; they have their exits and their entrances, and one man in his time plays many parts, his acts being seven ages...*
  William Shakespeare, Engish poet and playwright

With all due respect to Mr. Shakespeare, his poem seems to spiral downhill from here, in its negativity of his seven ages of life.

We do all have a story to tell however—A life story that is uniquely personal. If the world is a stage, and your life is live action, would you know your life purpose by the acts in your production? Would an audience? Is your life congruent—is what you believe reflected by the actions you take?

In ACT ONE: YOUR LIFE STORY, you embody the starring role. Act One is the play of your present and future life, and through it you will loosely and freely take a creative trip through your life experience. ACT ONE is like your own, personal dramafest. It provides you a theatrical framework in forming your own playbook.

Your playbook will help you discover hidden motivations behind your actions, and reveal important self-knowledge. This information will assist you in designing your life purpose, direction, and future success. When you use more and more of your natural talents and strengths in areas that interest you, you will succeed more often, and increase your happiness and satisfaction in life.

In your portfolio, begin now to design your own life story using the *Act One: Your Life Story* framework.

ACT ONE: YOUR LIFE STORY

Life isn't play practice, it's LIVE ACTION!

LIVE ACTION—Set Your Life Stage in 10 Exciting Steps

1. Lifestyle: SET—Paint a backdrop mural about yourself—how you want to lead your life. What's your scenery? Weigh decisions about the values you wish to include and how prominent a place each will take in your set (i.e., love, home, work, your favorite place, freedom, peace, time…). Next, bring on the joy, add details that make you happy (consider what, where, and who contribute to your happiness). It's your choice and focus…you set the stage!

2. Inspiration: CAST OF CHARACTERS—Bring your stage to life with your people: family, friends, colleagues, even villains (those who pose challenges or roadblocks for you).

3. Vision: PLOT—see your end result, the big picture, keep your eye on your path, even as you weave your story with all its twists and turns.

4. Energy: YOUR SCENES—ACTION! What are your exciting life events? Where do you find your inspiration? What is your greatest desire? What are you doing when you give your best performance?

5. Absorption: DRESS REHEARSALS! Costumes, makeup, props, tools, gadgets, accessories, equipment, accoutrements of your interests, comforts, and supports which engage you and enrich your performance.

6. Creative Peak: YOUR MOTIVATION AND TENSION—the good kind of tension, immersion in what you're doing, flow, your best and brightest ideas, the creative process of your life, the climax of the scenes of your life.

7. Triggers: YOUR CURTAIN CALLS—TO ACTION. Lights, Music, Cues. Move your story along. Make your details and actions mean something.

8. Inner Checkpoint: YOU ARE DIRECTOR—What scenes need more rehearsal? Ensure time management includes engagement in joyful scenes and activities front and center, and stage managing behind the scenes.

9. Outer Checkpoint: YOUR AUDIENCE—TAKE A BOW—Your impact on family, friends, job, community, by stepping out into the world, being brave, and taking positive action.

10. Notebook: ASSIMILATE YOUR PLAYBOOK—organization of your personal portfolio; completing the blueprint plan encompassing all of your great ideas that bring a smile to your face; resulting in successful creations and earnest living. Place problematic behavior permanently offstage.

CHAPTER 11: ACT ONE: YOUR LIFE STORY

Lights. Camera. Action!

- *In my plays, I want to look at life—at the commonplace of existence—as if we had just turned a corner and run into it for the first time.*
Christopher Fry, English poet and playwright

Chapter 12: Hope Chests and Tool Boxes

TOOLBOXES AND HOPE CHESTS FOR PERSONAL AND PROFESSIONAL DEVELOPMENT

What's In Your Hope Chest?

Advertisers and copywriters call their professional toolbox their "swipe file," a collection of advertising brochures and letters that have been proven to be successful, to inspire ideas.

Called a *Glory Box* in Australia, a hope chest is traditionally used for gathering household goods and heirlooms for a prospective bride. Also commonly known as a trousseau until the 1950s, a hope chest exemplifies a coming-of-age rite of passage for women. It sometimes holds part of a dowry for a young woman. At one point, pre-World War I, portability became an issue, and the chest wasn't a chest at all, but a calico bag holding household belongings, easy to transport.

For many women, collecting things in their hope chests remain pure joy. When they lift the lid on that trunk or box, they feel a connection: a sense of the past, a link to the present, and hope for the future. A hope chest represents the owner's dreams.

Your symbolic hope chest will be like that, a place to remind you of your hope, though perhaps a bit more gritty—a working girl's personal and professional toolbox.

It won't be a literal toolbox, unless that's what you want, but a large beautiful box or chest that holds your special mementos, linens, clothing, accessories, travel memories, photos, trinkets, or snips of paper you have cut out of magazines and newspapers for reasons only you know.

Place in your hope chest whatever wakes up your senses, and makes you happy; treasures that help you pick up the paintbrush or pen, take out your sewing machine and fabrics, or sit down at your computer and begin. The things in this chest of wonders will inspire one person only—you.

If you don't already have this type of hope chest, start one. It can be a lot of fun—and it's important. Creative people with ideas are not always in life reinforced for these talents. This hope chest isn't for anyone else, it's for you, and about you. It's what flicks your switch on. The things other people treasure are not the same as what you treasure. Your personality and interests should be all over it.

Tools for Setbacks: Slip Sliding Away

Some days you might feel like diving under the covers, as if dampened by rain, or overwhelmed by a storm. When this happens, ask yourself simply: what's going on? Are you overworked? Is there too much on your plate? Do you feel like you're juggling too many balls, and they all might fall if you stop? Are you afraid of something? Are you missing part of what you need to get over the hump? Do you procrastinate? Are you trying to cope with a chronic state or condition?

If you are finding it hard to stay on track, and seemingly small strays from your ideas and creative plans are increasing, then here are a few ways to reduce or stop ineffective patterns of behavior:

1. Create a great plan. Keep it simple and to the point. Realize that diversions from your schedules and plans have an impact on your life. They take something away from you—like time, energy, or well-being. It takes more effort to start over and build momentum again than it does to stay the course. So stay the course you set for yourself when at all possible. You've set your priorities, and they matter.

For example: An at-home mother of a large family had, over time, taken on the equivalent of more than a halftime job in volunteering for her children's school. When she realized that this much time defeated her purpose in desiring to stay home to raise her children and teach them the skills of farm living, she said no to project requests more often and found a better balance for herself and her family.

2. Take a short break. Breaks throughout the day keep you sharp when you return to your work.

3. Take a long break once in a while. Do you take a yearly vacation? Travel? How often do you "get away from it all?" Trips are important, even if it's a day trip or a weekend trip for a change of scenery. They keep you from getting stale, bored, or in a rut. Everybody needs a fresh perspective from time to time.

4. Seek and give support. Do you have the emotional support you need? Who can you call on for assistance? How do you develop and maintain a network of family, friends, business associates? People need time and nurturing, just like you. If you want people to be there for you when you

need them, you have to give relationships time, thought, and attention too.

- *People are like stained-glass windows. They sparkle and shine when the sun is out, but when the darkness sets in, their true beauty is revealed only if there is light from within.*
Elizabeth Kubler-Ross, Swiss American psychiatrist and author

Thomas Edison had much to say about staying the course in daily living. Here are a few of his gems:

- *Many of life's failures are people who did not realize how close they were to success when they gave up... Our greatest weakness lies in giving up. The most certain way to succeed is always to try just one more time...I have not failed. I've just found 10,000 ways that won't work.*

- *Opportunity is missed by most people because it is dressed in overalls and looks like work.*

- *The three essentials to achieve anything worthwhile are: hard work, stick-to-itiveness, and common sense.*

Thomas Edison, American inventor and businessman

Tools for Positive Daily Choices

YOUR CLOCK

Every day offers new opportunities to choose how you want to spend your time and energy. Begin to see your clock differently.

Time is a cycle of blocks of hours that you manage. When you manage your hours, you will become more acutely aware of the choices you make during the course of every day. If your hours slip away, you can't get them back. If you immerse yourself in each planned hour, your production will reward you.

GOOD CHOICE CYCLE EXERCISE

In your portfolio draw a large circle. Above the circle, write Good Choice Cycle. At the top of the circle, write down your very best quality, the quality that brings you joy; the one really good thing you do, or are developing, of which you are unreservedly most proud. That's the number one thing on your own personal Good Choice Cycle.

Moving clockwise, continue to add good qualities in decreasing order of the strength of their goodness in your life, until you get to the bottom of the circle.

The second half of the circle represents your less desirable tendencies or habits. At the bottom of your circle, write a habit that is not the worst you possess, but still not very good. Continuing clockwise, continue around the circle listing your progressively bad tendencies, until you are back near the top of your circle.

Now, between each of your progressively bad entries, put a bold dash. These dash lines represent the progression points at which you become aware of your less-than-ideal behavior. When you begin to approach your undesirable habits, this awareness will allow you to stop them cold, thus eliminating them that time, and replacing them with positive behavior.

Keep working your way back up the circle counterclockwise to form new and better habits. Perhaps one day your circle will be filled with mainly positive things.

This awareness tool is a great way to break any bad tendencies or habits, and become more frequently aware of creating better habits to replace the old ones. Use a new circle for each area of your life that you wish to improve upon.

For example, if you are trying to lose weight, and do well during the day without any problem, but you find that you are a night snacker, your circle would identify the problem. Let's say at 8:00 p.m. you begin snacking when a favorite television show comes on. Your awareness could lead you to change the snack to a low-cal one, like fresh vegetables instead of chips or ice cream, and increase your success in achieving self-discipline and/or weight loss. Also, mute the food ads.

If you're a midnight snacker, simply go to bed earlier than usual. You will wake up refreshed and ready to go, and not be disappointed with yourself for going off your plan the night before.

Take your control back.

- *We are what we repeatedly do. Excellence, then, is not an act, but a habit.*
  Aristotle, Greek philosopher

- *You can't wait for inspiration. You have to go after it with a club.*
  Jack London, American author, journalist, and activist

Tools for Appreciation and Gratitude

To live with gratitude is an awesome way to live. Who all in your life do you appreciate? When did you last thank them? How do you give credit where credit is due? What do you do to show your appreciation for your support team? How long has it been since you have written a thank-you note? Is it time to throw a dinner party or take someone to lunch?

What manner of success have you enjoyed in your creative journey of life? Do you make time every day to do what you love? Seize your opportunities, and savor the moments in them.

By now, your portfolio is brimming full of exciting ideas that are creative, innovative, and entirely you. Congratulations! Carry on!

- *There is only one of you in all time, this expression is unique. And if you block it, it will never exist through any other medium and it will be lost.*
  Martha Graham, American dancer, choreographer

Additional titles by Helen Hein are available at
amazon.com/author/helenhein

NONFICTION

Secrets of a Successful Quilt Club, A Ministry Model

Ideas, For Women Only, The Art of a Personal Portfolio (condensed)

Ideas, For Women Only, The Art of a Personal Portfolio:

Book One: Identify Your Talents

Book Two: Time Management

Book Three: Problems and Solutions

Book Four: Creative Collaborations

Book Five: The Great Balancing Act

Book Six: Successful Role Models

Book Seven: Motivation Magic

Book Eight: Self-Discovery

Book Nine: Transforming Moments

Book Ten: The Direction of Your Dreams

Book Eleven: Act One: Your Life Story

Book Twelve: Hope Chests and Toolboxes

FICTION

A COUNTRY PLACE novel

Cover Illustration by Ruth Doumit

TWO MINUTES OF HEAVEN short story

Cover Illustration by Linda Jacobus, www.lindasart.com

About the Author

HELEN HEIN, a Pacific Northwest author, poet, and artist, holds a Master of Arts Degree in Educational Psychology, and a Bachelor of Arts Degree in Communications. She worked several years as a mental health counselor, assisting families, teens, and children. Church work followed, as a pastoral staff minister for faith formation. Her first book, *A COUNTRY PLACE*, a contemporary love story and inspirational novel, is available in both traditional and e-book formats.

Currently, she writes on ideas, creativity, and life planning in a fast-moving world, with the 12 E-book Series: *IDEAS FOR WOMEN ONLY, The Art of a Personal Portfolio*. Her uplifting short stories, like *TWO MINUTES OF HEAVEN,* offer hope for hectic lives. The success of starting up her church quilt club inspired her to share how to do it. Don't miss her short e-book, *SECRETS OF A SUCCESSFUL QUILT CLUB, A Ministry Model.*

Married since 1980, with a grown son and daughter, she grew up on a large beef ranch with eight brothers and two sisters, the ninth of eleven children.

About the Cover Illustrator

LINDA JACOBUS is owner of Linda's Witness in Art, Classical Realism Oil Paintings by Linda Jacobus. Linda was born in Palo Alto, California, and was raised in Saratoga until the age of eleven, eventually moving to Martinez, California with her family of six sisters and one brother. Linda married and has four precious sons. In 2003, she and her husband moved to the beautiful Northwest, where she still resides.

Throughout her life, Linda had been searching to fill an unknown void. In 1992, she picked up a brush and stroked the canvas, knowing then that the void had been filled. She is a self-taught artist and loves to study as much as she loves to paint. Being self-taught has enabled her to accomplish techniques in which she can freely express herself. She considers herself a tonalist, and enjoys depicting the unique degrees of value. Most of all, she loves to capture the light that shines upon the subject and the shadows that bring forth the light.

Linda has won awards and has paintings throughout the country and abroad. In Linda's words, "I have come to the conclusion that what I paint God has created, I just copy His works. He is my teacher."